CLIMB PARNASSUS, AND BEHOLD!

*Elisabeth Stückgold-von Veress, later Frau Steffen,
with her daughter Felizitas Stückgold.*

CLIMB PARNASSUS, AND BEHOLD!

Poems
by
ALBERT STEFFEN

Translated
by
DAISY ALDAN

ADONIS PRESS
Hawthorne Valley, Ghent, N.Y.

Acknowledgments:

Thanks to Ili Hackländer for her valuable collaboration and to
Ingeborg Maresca and Dr. Friedrich Behrmann
for their suggestions.

Cover arranged by Barbara Richey

ISBN 0-932776-20-5

Published with permission from Verlag für Schöne
Wissenschaft — Dornach, Switzerland

CONTENTS   PAGE NO.

NO MANDATE WAS GIVEN TO ME

No mandate was given to me, not from gods
and not from men:
dictum from no one was ordained for me.
I knew not from where I had come,
nor where I would go:
In the place of my birth I found myself:
father, mother, brothers around me:
the garden, the field, the wood,
far off, the mountains.
Soon one thing I perceived, but by myself:
I would be true, aware of beauty, do good deeds.
For this I had many as ideal
and I loved them.
From them I could learn,
of works of divine olden times,
how to explore, how to test, how to pursue them;
that was my will, not another's.
No teacher commanded - You must!
And if someone did, I questioned,
did what I felt right.
So looking around me,
I beheld the earthrealm:
stones, plants, beasts, and the stars.
All beings conversed with me,
and I sought to embrace them.
Of each I learned something,
of myself but little,
until I perceived myself
as a Stranger, from the view of my higher being.
At first the world seemed to be good,
then I saw that some things were evil.
Beauty, I thought, was in all men's souls,
and many I beheld so ugly.

I sought for truth
and found the lie:
evil, ugliness, lie:
I longed to transform them.
That's why I struggled with others
when they did not grant me the freedom
to see, to declare and to do
what I perceived to be true and good and beautiful.
I was deigned to love the Christ
for He compelled me to nothing.
He became my highest Master.
All others were so only,
insofar as they declared:
'Not I, but Christ in me'.
But the night which leads to the void?
I learned from the darkness longing for light.
Light engenders the colors through darkness.
Color awakens the soul.
The soul learns from the stars
the words of the gods.
The primal truth they taught me
was this:

Man, you are free, and, Man, you may love;
Man, know yourself destined for freedom,
ever born again out of love,
to work as one in communion with all.
That is your mandate, granted to you by yourself,
right for those who are free, and who love.

CLIMB PARNASSUS, AND BEHOLD

Behold there all the butterflies,
butterflies upon the blossoms,
on the blossoms of your soul,
of your soul, full-fledged for spirit.

Spirit: dove, freed from the body,
dove who flies to the Christ Jesus,
the Christ Jesus, Son of God,
Son of God, unto the Savior,
to the Savior, leads toward Fish.

Fish in ocean of the world,
ocean of the world, once heaven,
heaven changed to purest warmth,
purest warmth to light-full breath,
light-full breath to clearest water,
clearest water to firm ice.

Ice, that melts in flame of heart
flame of heart of hallowed love,
hallowed love, now resurrected,
resurrected out of ashes,
out of ashes of the phoenix,
Phoenix-I on Mount Parnassus
Climb Parnassus, and behold!

ROCKY QUADRANT

Rocky quadrant,
water whorls,
airy columns,
light in spirals:
They all lead me
to the world where reign the senses.
I perceive there
in the beasts,
in the plants,
in the stones:
My own being in them all
and in me all earthly death.

Body dying,
carcass wasting,
soul refining,
spirit winging:
Hands of Gods
lift me high and heavenward.
Cosmic wisdom,
Angel-glances,
breath of life,
blessed by the Christ:
Resurrected
I take part in world creation.

YOU STONE, YOU PLANT, AND YOU O BEAST

You stone, you plant, and you O beast, — I am
not you, yet know myself as with you born:
on the path to selfhood I left you forlorn:
you call: in longing I turn back; I hear.

A counterforce thinks, speaks and wills to tear
me from the goal that I was chosen for;
to wrest me from the Hours and the shelter
of world creation in its primal form.

And should I fail to find you in me now,
in space as star, in flow of time, as I
ally myself once more with all God's creatures,
it is in vain I say: I know myself.

As I ascended, so I caused your fall
I bow before you; raise you to the All.

EYE, VAULTED LIKE THE HEAVENS

Eye, vaulted like the heavens,
toward which it gazes,
perceives in the mirror of soul
the heavenly Sons,
surrounding the Table of Sun.

A shadow in the ring of light
makes it suddenly see
that one has abandoned the Table,
descended to earth,
to lead homeward through colors
those fallen a prey to the darkness.

Eye, refined in the rainbow of tears,
illumines the path on high,
the Dead in the dark, blue-paling; yellow-paling in light,
losing themselves in the gloom.
Angels bestow on it strength
to guide them in the labyrinth of woe.

Eye, transformed to remembrance,
perceiving, countries and cities,
with temples, palaces, tents, houses and huts,
with marketplace and the arena
and the dungeons under the earth.

Pulsebeat and breath become outcry.
Wavering steps along graves.
Death descends in the sight-realm.
But the Son of the Sun overcomes him!

Eye, that is graced by the Spirit...

THE EYE GLORIFIED

Man spoke
as he looked up to the cosmos,
which as eternal, is vaulted
over the head, from whose thought, life flees:
"Not the mortal self
but may the Heavenly Being
who attained resurrection
on the Mount of Skulls
reign in my being."

But what the Heavenly Being
endured in the mortal ego
remained concealed.

And the Man spoke further to himself:
"All that I experience
in my mortal body
must be transformed.
Let me, guardian of my bodily form,
which through you, will not perish,
discern whether I am nothing to you
in the way I appear to myself
as the mortal 'I'."

But the Heavenly Being answered him thus:
"You, O Man, are the eye,
through which from the All, I looked down,
as Son of the Sun,
to lead home to the Father
earthly humanity destined for death.
In this way I behold in Man
the paths to the Creator.
I would behold every grief,
weakness, sickness and death,

path of error, abyss,
blindness of soul, ever newly devised,
as the fallen Angel
once brought to existence.
And so I have come
to bring you once more the light of the spirit."

"Yes,"
the man gravely vowed:
"Refined through you
In the darkness of mortal substance
I will follow the call to awake.
I will lead Lucifer to the Savior's Spirit,
for now I can fathom your thoughts,
Heavenly Being, even in the mortal 'I'.
You bring the world creations
home to the heart of the Creator.
— Therefore you endow the animals with wings
as guardians in moonlight.
— Therefore you sow in me through conscience
the innocence of flowers;
and you transport me to the sun.
— Therefore you would mold into a star
the earth in me,
with all of earth's stone.

Beholder of the Creation, I may be your eye:
Tool ordained by myself
to bring once again
through your grace
heavenly essence
within the mortal 'I'!"

DEW OF THE ROSE

Dew of the Rose!
Out-breathed night,
in-breathed day.
Prime-tone of light,
rune in space.
Aum at morning,
Amen at evening.

Eagle-transmuted Word!
Between the wings reposes
sleeping, the mortal 'I'.
Life-awakening breath,
spirit-purified love
lifts the fading image
high to the radiant-Being.

Self awakens in selfhood!
Gifted with cosmic eyes,
mortal earth I behold
resurrected as star.

FROM THE EYES, FROM OUT THEIR GLEAMING

From the eyes, from out their gleaming
does the Spirit fetch its colors,
so it may portray its angels.
From the life-force in its thinking
love itself creates the pinion
to accompany the dead.
From the truth in recollection
memory builds up the temple
where it may revere the gods.

In the breath of heaven's greeting
the heart hears the sounds of Sun
sung by the disciple-circle.
In red nectar of grape clusters
mouth tastes hallowed nourishment
which the Risen One bestowed.
In the substance of the body
foot perceives earth gravity,
that which tethers it to deeps.

Through the fire of his passions
willing senses its opponent
brought to birth within himself.
Through the conscience' admonition
beings weave upon his goals,
and direct him to Creator.
Through the fate that creatures suffer
destiny achieves fulfillment
in compassion, in redemption.

AYE AND AMEN!

Aye and Amen!
So say I to all creations of life,
since when, O friend, I found you in Spring,
like the blossoms, the children of the Sun,
yourself as child;
then as woman, who redeemed through love;
bound like the sheaves of Summer,
prepared for the bread;
now as mother, the child in her arms,
but by destiny ploughed like the bare land,
visited hard by the storms of Autumn;
and lastly, as a nun of the hallowed sorrows.
Soul landscapes always hovered around you,
mountains of hope, lakes of sacrifice
and the primal tone of the source, consolation of dews,
transforming dark into light.
And I love, O companion, all things through you.
Once I went seeking my Self
in the beings of the cosmos.
Now I perceive you in the place of eternal being.
There dwells the sanctified faith.
Why are we deemed worthy of such heavenly homeland?
Because we declare:
Not we, but Christ in us.

CHILD WITH HEAVEN WITHIN YOU

Child with heaven within you.
Your great soul looked out of your wide eyes;
the delicate body collided with the world around it,
so it might become aware of your essence.
You were granted encounter with mankind's creator,
but also with the foul destroyers of his works.
Innocence must know guilt in the very core of its body.
Through the offering you became ill
and you knew not the reason.
But always you said: "I wish to get well to help others."
It was this which so saddened your eyes.
The very last words you breathed
conquered your pain:
"I know not, I know not, — "
a smile full of light
which encircled your mother,
" — how I can be so blissful."
— It was, that the Angel of Death
gave you his love...

EARLY DEATH

Soul,
which was like the mountain spring,
gliding over granite rocks,
and springing from primal earth times,
through cosmic refinement
no longer darkened
from the burial grounds here below,
without having lost the tempestuous force of youth!
— What lightning formerly wielded in her;
how then the thunder rolled,
that all became singing, and was so mighty,
it shattered the delicate body
so like an amphora
borne by angels.
Rapture, enchantment, ecstasy
of heavenly longing raised her high
in the sinking day's
steadily soaring crimson fire.
But the heads of the mountains turned pale,
and the midnight sun
carried the blessed one home.

PERSEPHONE

Persephone
I am more devoted to you than before
and yet more sundered;
A dead man already,
thus I feel though alive,
who have no strength to reach your heart again
because his own weighs so heavy.
How like a wound the world has now become,
which once was young in Spring; for me no longer.
I seem to be a spirit on a star.
The bird among the branches calls the dead,
the flowers blossom out of blood,
which drips down on the stem of the crucifix.
The soul lives in all blossoming.
The body bleeds to death in pain.
As I pursue my way alone
upon this path of torment,
the little lame foot of a child I know
appears to me in thought.
Innocence that suffers, grant me strength
so I may nevermore forget
through my own griefs,
that I am called
to share
in the Redeemer's work.

UPON AN ISLAND

Upon an island lying in the ocean
upon whose shore-seam made of sand of shells,
oases of blue blossoms flower;
The child who died so young encounters you
and deeply grieving, speaks:
"You shall portray star-images of blossoms
and bring them to my Angel.
He will reveal my fate to you,
and how the innocent and mortal body
could be attacked by pain as great as this."

The Angel took your image
which seemed
breathed forth from water and from spirit.
Then pointed to the distant continent
of Hellas, and spoke thus:
"The pillared temples fell
but Christ arose.
The feebleness of suffering
is nearer
to the Redeemer, who was crucified
and then descended to the Underworld
to free Persephone..."

He lifts the child unto Himself...

THUNDER-ECHO OF APPROACHING WORLD
   TEMPEST

Thunder-echo of approaching world tempest,
resounding on skull-roof,
drumming whirlwind of circling shank bones
on taut stretched skins.
Dust of ground crystals oozes down from the brow,
spectral exhalings of anguish.
Empty soundings of fractured god-discourses:
Theos, Tiox, Izan...

Shadow races wander by:
heads, coxcomb-helmeted,
Bodies, clothed in hanging tigerskins
shrunken limbs like desert birds.
Eden — rabid do they dance:
Atta, Nacky, Naret...

Captive, lashed, in savage woe,
they rush headlong into flight
to the breakers of the Five Gates
on the coastline of the Oceans,
to the moon, imploring help,
upward, high, they raise their hands:
Eke, Sider, Sul...

On the far horizon nears
now the golden Navicella
with the Light-form of the Savior,
and He sings a song of Sun,
joins the syllables, free of sins,
once again to cosmic Word,
which abode in each one's heart,
from the world beginning: Alpha,
to the ending: Omega,
speaks the Risen One — the Christ.

NOW IS THE HOUR

Now is the hour for farewell to life,
not from friends whom I shall never lose,
for I will find them again after I die.
But from you, stones, plants and beasts.
Longing for loftier visions will take hold of me
for spheres of purity and songs of gods.

Not for long may I hold in my hands
this crystal with light-flooded rims,
primal image enclosing the secret of mountains.
— However, the eagle who abides in the rocks
ravages on when the head falls to dust
if you fail to return.

Soon the source springing from glaciers will no longer
      refresh me
flowing to blue-lake, surrounded by mountain meadows,
primal waters transforming to rivers and oceans.
— But the seasonal flowers which grow on the shore
are poisoned when the heart becomes cold
if you fail to return.

Already in breathing, awareness leaves me;
dead are the thoughts which through colors awoke
prime-tone of sounds — estranged far from hearing.
— But the words of creation die in the body,
corpses placed on your own dead body
if you fail to return.

I'll find freedom from earthly life at last,
which the fall of mankind bequeathed to me,
primal fall, my own, but never can I forget
that there below the ego-forsaken
still abide. I seek the Redeemer
to follow Him *there*, singing the song of mankind.

BY THE WINGS OF WEAVING WOMEN

By the wings of weaving women,
who the zodiacal tapestry embroider,
is the joyful dancer, feather-light,
led away so she, herself, may weave
the life-trace of her soles into the fabric,
Destiny she paced within her body,
now is covered by a funeral shroud,
which will be delivered up to fire.
Now her spirit grasps the script of traces
of her graceful moving feet once more,
to convey it to the cosmic chronicle,
bearing the corrections which the Fates
of her destiny must now impose.

Dance, they say, upon this tapestry,
you yourself, have woven, from the Virgin
to the Scales, unto the Scorpion,
straight to Sagittarius, who will shield you
with his arrows from the minotaur.

There among the leafless silver branches
where the bird Simurgh is perched and sings,
unicorn awaits, looks to the branches;
you ride forth on him to the Child of Sun,
who at midnight of the world was born.

DEEP IN THE NIGHT

The greed of Hell's hyenas
is rapacious.
They fatten on the soul-cadavres of the dead.
Dreadful that the living beings follow,
who while still in the body, decay.

But you turn your gaze aloft
to the star-chariot.
Be seated therein,
the beast will not follow you there.

How lovely here those who have died!
The angels of blossoms have lifted from their shoulders
the weights of the beasts.
They dwell now in colors of asters.
Do you feel how they ray forth,
golden, purple and blue?

GUILTY, DECLARED THE JUDGE

Guilty, declared the judge
in judging the innocent man.
On unjust judgment thrived
the community of the accuser.
What then does the heart which breaks?
It forgives and now
it becomes an eye of Spirit,
looks out into the spheres
and there encounters a countenance
full of Love divine.
Whose? — The Comforter.

"I have hunger," spoke the dancer.
The priest then offered her the sickle-chalice,
the wheaten bread within as shadow-body.
She turned aside, and in the movement showed
a Tao: — "Only death stills my desire."

CEASE YOUR SORROW

Cease your sorrow. Every woe
one day from an angel will be
lifted up, so you may vanquish,
that for which you shed these tears.

And the angel then will carry
in his arms this suffering;
tell of it to Guide of Fate
and transform it within time.

When the stars translumine it,
it may be a source of healing,
for all who in future ages
find themselves again on earth.

INSTEAD OF USELESS COMPLAINING

Instead of useless complaining
that no one supports him,
that no one inspires to deeds,
from nowhere appears consolation,
the desolate man listens
to the mundane clamor,
bewildering rumblings of suns in explosion.
Yet, in the distant thunder
he perceives melodious sounds,
the word of one dead,
from ascending star of the evening.
This soul still loves you,
and love is near
even in loneliest night.

YOU MUST VENTURE OUT

You must venture out,
not only from house and home:
that is never enough.
The time is for loftier flight,
with valiant wings!
What weaving in the heights of snow:
from there heaven wills to reflect
itself on your brow.
Within your thoughts there speaks
the Light of World: I am!
Now you may dare.
The Spirit will bear you.

On the light-ray which in darkness falls,
is inscribed your very name.
There above, the sun who calls it,
there below, the soul who hears it.
Word incarnate, lets you hear
how the whole world's language is intoned.

OH, MAN, YOU ASK

Oh, Man, you ask:
Is Christ as sad as I?
In you sad, still more.

Is Christ as forsaken as I?
In you forsaken, still more.

Is Christ as helpless as I?
In you helpless, still more.

Is Christ as tormented as I?
In you tormented, still more.

Is Christ dying as I?
Resurrected from death is Christ
in all human beings, and loves them.
Love them, you also;
sad,
forsaken,
helpless,
tormented
unto death,
from whom Christ took the goad.

IN SLEEP OF SENSES

In sleep of senses, yet awake to spirit,
man sees himself within the realm of earth,
bound in on one side by the cross
and on the other by the empty grave.
And he perceives the path to resurrection,
descent to Hell, your destiny on earth.
Fulfill your fate and you will find the Christ.

YES, IT IS FOR MY GOOD

Yes, it is for my good
that I am confined to my room,
since my limbs bear me upright no longer.
But I can scale the tree by my window,
ascend it in spirit
as high as the stars,
which weave through the treetops
now in the moon-night —

The wandering planets
as destiny for me
glide through
the soul-nights
and shine for me brighter —

SPIRITS OF CHILDHOOD

Spirits of childhood,
you return to my aging body
and speak of becoming.
I feel again, as when a boy,
with bare feet I strode the gravel path,
waded through the brook
and leapt in the meadow;
joyous, I inhaled the breeze,
warmed myself in the sun.

God's love made Word
lives ever in me,
preserved in the dying body,
I thank life in death.

NAUGHT

Naught from outside,
Naught from inside,
nights and days and ever naught.
But within my '*I*', Alas!
anguish wakes through nullity
and groans.

Woe-sound stilled through harmony.
As a child it speaks to me,
lifts the nightmare from my heart,
Ah and *O*, breathes in my ear.
It resounds in light and love.
Wherefore does it bring me solace,
free me from the fear of death?

From on high reply intones:
"It is so because I died:
Resurrected in the Word,
from the All I come again."

"Why do you return to me?"

"It was you who loved my language
and you built a tent for me:
built it from the life-tree's fibre,
fetched the seats down from the stars,
placed them round the sun-gold table,
which you laid with crystal vessels
whereon was the soma drink:
The meal finished, all the sounds
those my children, those your guests,
guided into Eden-garden,
to the beasts, the winged ones

sleeping near the Tree of Knowledge.
And you wrote upon its leaves
verses, till they raised their heads.

Men and beasts and plants and stones
found themselves in poetry,
Aum as onset,
end as Amen,
in your 'I' renewed to life.
Go into the world and tell
to all beings what you witnessed:
I am between light and space,
outside,
inside,
and in me is all creation."

SAD MOOD

Sad mood — black web
weighs heavily.
Are these the dead, senselessly murdered,
heads decapitated with hatchets,
the hanged on the rope?

No more sufferers now.
But the murderers still in derision.
This is the bloody cloud
overshadowing the sky
so that the breath of God, I
no more can feel,
no more perceive
intonings of the stars.
Solace no longer descends from above
as dew on the eye,
which in its hollow expires.

Yet Christ dwells always within you.
Downward, not upward
may your spirit descend
now to the voyage to Hell
with Him together,
the One who has risen from death...

IN THE VOID OF THE HEAD

In the void of the head,
that no longer conceives thoughts
in the nightmare of the chest,
that strangles the breath,
in the weakness of the limbs
that can muster no strength to walk,
O, in the weariness of the whole body,
that no more will refresh
the springs of earthly life:
Only my body's
skeleton form holds me upright.
Through it, however, speaks to me Death:
    Yes!
You have ascended the steps
where the World-soul is crucified!
— And I see the Cross
growing on the earth-rim,
as the sun has set.
It raises itself
in the heights of heaven,
O sign of death!
But the stars revolve around the axis of the Cross
and intone:
Christ has risen from death!

YES, YOU ARE OLD

Yes, you are old.
But even were you young,
death would still be near you.
Mankind's suicide everywhere.
Therefore each one must ponder
in this hour: What do I do?
Hold on to what never can be destroyed.
The firm supports not.
The fluid forms not.
The airy bears not.
But the warmth — that I bring forth from the heart.
It weaves in the ether the pictures of life;
in those may I bide.
Yet, some become torment to me.
Those are the deeds through which I caused pain.
I ceaselessly ponder how to redeem them.
There streams from heart to the head
a spring which never runs dry.
I behold the earth transformed to a star.
Raying toward me from my head to my heart,
He who has risen!

A BEING OF WARMTH HOVERS

A being of warmth hovers
high above you
casting shadows in moonlight,
with feelers, which sense
what skeletal cold brings forth on earth:
Hate, which condenses to nightmare.

Like a roller, now it grows heavy,
is cleft in the middle;
streams pour forth to the depths,
to extinguish what mankind has blackened.
Lightning strikes,
it thunders,
upward ascends the abyss.
Now your shelter caves in.

But the Cherub who rises from there,
has wings of fire.
He speaks:
Conscience am I,
a messenger of Sun,
which Earth is destined to be.

Now warmth transforms to light.
The rainbow rays forth.

O HEART IN WHICH THE EARTHBOUND SENSE

O heart, in which the earthbound sense
now sinks. Now deeper darkens, wilder thunders
the blood; in its fall and rising I
myself design the pictures free from body:
spirals, circles, lemniscates
of path of gods which leads me to the Star
which is my origin; back to creative deeds;
back to the core of world-creation.

From there an Elohim invades my heart,
to lighten once again the body's dark,
the dark which Lucifer used as a nest;
he who had fallen and who then with hate
seduced with glittering illusion —
O heart, redeemed in radiance-ether-sea.

ON A SARCOPHAGUS

On a sarcophagus engraved
I notice tracings, and I read the sense:
the way I was before my present birth,
then death inherited.

Erected: Pillar, lemniscate and round.
A pair of wings then, which this form surrounds,
unfurls itself: I sink into the grave,
and now the mouth grows mute.

The Tao on the earth-sphere towering,
its wings embracing west and east,
dove-like comforter, the *Isis—Eye*,
the Spirit sheltering you.

BEYOND

Beyond: — The body is from ego severed,
as it beholds its own cast shadow,
fourfold, still enlivened by the elements
of life: of earth, of water, air and light.
Heat in the limbs, and ash within the face.
I was thus, this I know, and am not this.

Will I, transformed, once more become this I?
I see how rising from the crypt of death
appears a being who transrays the bone.
It is still dark within the tomb of skulls,
dead thoughts are haunting spectres in the air.
Spawn of the underworld makes light the cleft.

Burrows in the labyrinth of brain,
paints black and white in gleaming of the moon
and now the tapestry of silver threads
unravels, which the Fates of Death are sowing.
While ether exhalations weave about me,
I see myself descending to the earth.

Yet not on foot: I ride a Mount of Sun,
within my body — a gift of Helios — the Son.

FOR THE DEATH OF PERCY MACKAYE

A man attired in hierarchical robes
leads him from the foreign-city-tumult
there, where the Cathedral stood
which he so often visited in dreams;
points out to him the old familiar frescoes
in muted glimmer of stained-glass rosettas,
till they grow pale and change to arabesques
like silhouetted forms of skeletons.
Three times a knocking sounds within the grave-vault.
The light dies out. Death was his companion.
The Word transforms the structure of the bones.
The human frame rings forth in scales of stars.
The Poet joins him who prepares the Way
with consonants and vowels drawn forth from Heaven.

GOAL FOR COSMIC YEAR

Let our goal be this for cosmic year:
To create a painting for the soul,
which the claws of death may not despoil,
which illumines even darkest·dungeon,
and to bear with us an earth renewed,
which the shades of evil cannot fetter,
which will never perish in the floods,
which the raging winds can never pale,
nor corroding lye can ever poison,
which can never melt in heat of fire,
yet which still is brighter than the sun,
this is granted us by Christ alone.

WORKS BY ALBERT STEFFEN
AVAILABLE IN ENGLISH
and carried by the

ADONIS PRESS
Hawthorne Valley / Harlemville / Ghent, N.Y. 12075

ALBERT STEFFEN, an Anthology.
A comprehensive selection of Steffen's work, and tributes for his 75th birthday. Hardbound: gold Steffen design on white cloth. Adonis Press, 1959.   146pp.

MEETINGS WITH RUDOLF STEINER
An account of Steffen's impressions, insights and gratitude to Rudolf Steiner, experienced throughout many years; First Meetings; Remarks by Rudolf Steiner on the Conduct of Life, A Community of Builders, On Meditation, The Founding of the Weekly "Das Goetheanum," The Literature of the Future; Passages from Steffen's diaries; The Bridge between the Living and the Dead: A Turning Point in World History. Translated by Reginald Raab, Erna McArthur and Virginia Brett. Hardbound: gold lettering on purple cloth. *Verlag für Schöne Wissenchaften, Dornach, Switzerland, 1961.*   *344pp.*

FROM GEORGE ARCHIBALD'S LIFE STORY
& POSTHUMOUS PAPERS, *a novel, translated by Virginia Brett.*
A book intended especially for the West. George, after a humiliating failure and the inner wrestlings of adolescence, seeks out the suffering and the depraved in order to learn an understanding that can heal. Translated by Virginia Brett. Hardbound: gold Steffen design on purple cloth. *Verlag für Schöne Wissenschaften, 1961.*   270pp.

REMOLDING OF DESTINIES, short stories.
The characters and the fundamental forces at work within their lives are pictured with an extraordinary wealth of original detail. Old karma is resolved and reshaped into the beginnings of new destiny. Softbound: blue Steffen motif on plum color, arranged by Peter Stebbing. *Adonis Press,* second edition, 1984.   86pp.

DRAMAS
THE DEATH EXPERIENCE OF MANES
Scenes in Gondhishapur, Mesopotamia and Simurghia; the deeds and visions of Manes, and the victory of the spirit when the Manichaeans are surprised during their ritual and face destruction. Translated by Daisy Aldan, Elly Simmons and Virginia Brett. Hardbound: silver lettering on green. *Folder Editions,* New York and *Verlag für Schöne Wissenchaften,* Dornach, 1970.   105pp.

HIRAM AND SOLOMON, translated by Virginia Brett.
The tragic conflict and seeds for reconciliation between the descendants of Cain and Abel; the casting of the Brazen Sea in the Temple of Solomon. *Verlag für Schöne Wissenchaften,* 1970. Hardbound: gold lettering on red-violet cloth, $7.50.   Softbound: 90pp.

THE FALL OF ANTICHRIST, translated by Dora Baker and Daisy Aldan.
A dramatic sketch set in the future. A priest engineer and poet are pitted against the Regent, whose goal is to emancipate the earth and mankind from the spiritual cosmos. Softbound:white lettering on dark red. *Folder Editions,* New York.   52pp.

VOYAGE TO THE OTHER LAND, translated by Arviá MacKaye.
Scenes in an Egyptian tomb and in the salon and boiler room of the S.S. Titanic reflect forces at work in our civilization which strive towards titanic dimensions and are mysteriously connected with the culture of ancient Egypt. During the catastrophe, a group of passengers win insights whereby to build a ship of life which can bear them securely into the future. Hardbound: gold lettering on light blue cloth. *Verlag für Schöne Wissenchaften,* 1956. 122pp.

WORKS BY ALBERT STEFFEN AVAILABLE IN ENGLISH
and carried by the
ADONIS PRESS
Hawthorne Valley / Harlemville / Ghent, N.Y. 12075

DRAMAS (Continued)

ALEXANDER'S TRANSFORMATION, translated by Eleanor Trives.
Alexander's experiences, together with Aristotle, in the spiritual world after death, and their preparation for a new incarnation. Hardbound: gold Steffen design on white. *Verlag für Schöne Wissenchaften,* 1956.   122pp.

LIN, translation by Margaret Lloyd revised by Sophia Walsh.
Human tragedies in China arising from the Opium War and their implications for us today. Hardbound: blue lettering on yellow cloth. *Verlag für Schöne Wissenchaften,* 1956.
140pp.

ESSAYS

PILGRIMAGE TO THE TREE OF LIFE, translated by Eleanor Trives.
"A little book that lives ... Steffen is able to illuminate nature so that, through his wonderfully-wrought sentences, she lets the radiance of her mysteries shine back to us."

—Rudolf Steiner.

Frontispiece: Photograph of the author. Softbound: Steffen motif, mulberry on green, arranged by Peter Stebbing. *Adonis Press,* second edition 1978.   66pp.

THE ARTIST BETWEEN WEST AND EAST: THE PATH OF THE POET
Dostoyevsky's *Brothers Karamazov* leaves unsolved questions. How shall the poet answer them? "Never before did the poet stand in such danger of being swept away. A twofold tempest threatens him from both sides... 'For myself,' says the poet, 'I seek my master in my own being.' ~ And who shall be my guide?' ~ Nature!'"   — *Albert Steffen* Translated by Reginald E. Raab. *Adonis Press,* 1946. Hardbound: gold label on deep blue, $5.00.   Softbound: 84pp.

RACE, FOLK, INDIVIDUALITY AND MANKIND, translated by
Arvia MacKaye.
The mysteries of Advent and of the Three Kings in the light of the consciousness soul. Softbound: red lettering on buff. *Adonis Press,* second edition, 1982.   30pp.

MYSTERY-DRAMA FROM ANCIENT TO MODERN TIMES, arranged
by Erna Grund.
Origin of the Drama; Sophocles as a Poet of the Mysteries; The Iphigenia of Euripides and Goethe; Dante's Style; Shakespeare; The Way Forward in Dramatic Art; Signpost to a New Mystery-Drama; From a Notebook. Translated by Virginia Brett and Christa Macbeth. Illustrated by photographs of scenes from Steffen's dramas. Softbound: Steffen motif, orange on light blue, arranged by Peter Stebbing. *Adonis Press,* 1977.   40pp.

ADDRESS AT THE DEDICATION OF THE GOETHEANUM
WEST WINDOW, translated by Virginia Brett.
The Michaelic themes and colors of the Goetheanum windows in the midst of modern forces directed towards "total war, tyranny and terrorism." Delivered at Michaelmas, 1945. Softbound: gold lettering on deep blue. *Verlag für Schöne Wissenchaften,* 1966.
26pp.

THE DETERMINATION OF EVIL, translated by Daniel Marston.
The Determination of Evil; The Gorgon Head; The Knowing Eye; The Hearing Heart. Translated especially for Steffen's Centennial. Softbound: large format, black lettering on orange. *Verlag für Schöne Wissenchaften,* 1984.   18pp.

42

WORKS BY ALBERT STEFFEN AVAILABLE IN ENGLISH
and carried by the
ADONIS PRESS
Hawthorne Valley / Harlemville / Ghent, N.Y. 12075

POEMS

IM ANDERN LAND — IN ANOTHER LAND
Poems inter-translated by Albert Steffen and Percy MacKaye. Hardbound: gold Steffen design on white. *Verlag für Schöne Wissenchaften*, 1937.   60pp.

SELECTED POEMS OF ALBERT STEFFEN, translated by Daisy Aldan.
Poems chosen from four of Steffen's books of verse. German and English on facing pages. Softbound: white lettering on purple. *Folder Editions*, New York, 1968.   70pp.

STEFFEN, verses translated by Virginia Brett.
Poems for which Rudolf Steiner created eurythmy forms.   *Verlag Walter Keller*, Dornach, Switzerland.   54pp.

FROM A NOTEBOOK, second edition, translated by Arvia MacKaye.
Aphorisms and short passages that throw light on the nature of language and individual destiny in ways that bring help, healing and health.

THE CRISIS IN THE LIFE OF THE ARTIST, second edition, translated by Arvia MacKaye.
Two essays that kindle enthusiasms for taking new steps in all the arts, especially in the arts of dealing with life, illness and destiny.

LITTLE MYTHS, translated by various writers.
"Often I am asked how my 'Little Myths' come into being.... I find them, to my own astonishment, on the way to the spirit, like precious stones, trees, birds, like a perspective of clouds and rainbows....but always otherwise than I had supposed in advance before I had walked the path of knowledge."   — Albert Steffen
Illustrations and cover arranged by Van James.

NEW BEGINNING, Freedom and Love in the Crisis of Modern Consciousness.
Selections from *The Mission of Poetry*, translated by Arvia MacKaye Ege.
"Steffen's attitude towards the world and man is one of self-education through transformation....In this sense his life work became a therapeutic deed....The words and images in which these insights and harkenings are expressed stand there in simple beauty, without pretense. Through them wafts, as delicately as a breath of color, hidden rhythms and melodies which place the spiritual reality before the soul in its purest clarity." — Karl Ege

POEMS, an Anthology of translations by various poets.

STEFFEN'S WORKS IN THE ORIGINAL GERMAN

(14 novels, 14 sketches and miniatures, 11 books of poetry, 16 dramas, 18 volumes of essays)
may be ordered from
Verlag für Schöne Wissenchaften, Albert Steffen Stiftung, 4143 Dornach, Switzerland

---

Write to ADONIS PRESS for information of assorted Steffen post cards and small prints in color. Large portfolios available through St. George Book Service.

Please add $1 for postage and handling of one book and 35¢ for each additional book, enclose your check made out to ADONIS PRESS, and send your order to
ADONIS PRESS, Hawthorne Valley, Harlemville, Ghent, N.Y. 12075

43

WORKS BY ALBERT STEFFEN

Novels:
Ott, Alois and Werelsche. 1907.
Die Bestimmung der Roheit. 1912.
Die Erneuerung des Bundes. 1913.
Der rechte Liebhaber des Schicksals. 1916.
Sibylla Mariana. 1917.
Lebensgeschichte eines jungen Menschen. 1928.
Wildeisen. 1929.
Sucher nach sich selbst. 1931.
Aus Georg Archibalds Lebenslauf und nachgelassenen Schriften. 1950.
Oase der Menschlichkeit. 1954.
Altmanns Memoiren aus dem Krankenhaus. 1956.
Dreiunddreissig Jahre. 1959.
Die Mission der Poesie. 1962.

Elisabeth Steffen / Selbstgewähltes Schicksal Mit Gedenkworten von Albert Steffen. 1961.

Remembrances, sketches and miniatures
Kleine Mythen. 1923.
Pilgerfahrt zum Lebensbaum. 1925.
In Memoriam Rudolf Steiner. 1925.
Lebenswende. 1931.
Merkbuch. 1937.
Buch der Rückschau. 1938.
Selbsterkenntnis und Lebenschau. 1940.
Auf Geisteswegen. 1942.
Der Genius des Todes. 1943.
Novellen. 1947.
Aus der Mappe eines Geistsuchers. 1951.
Gedenkbilder für Elisabeth Steffen. Mit zwölf farbigen Aquarellwiedergaben. 1961.

Lebensbilder an der Todespforte. Mit zwölf farbigen
    Aquarellwiedergaben. 1963.
Reisen hüben und drüben. Mit vierzehn farbig
    wiedergegebenen Skizzen. 1963.

Poems

Wegzehrung. 1921.
Gedichte. 1931.
Der Tröster. 1935.
Passiflora / Ein Requiem für Felicitas. 1939.
Wach auf, du Todesschläfer. 1941.
Epoche. 1944.
Spätsaat. 1947.
Am Kreuzweg des Schicksals. 1952.
Krankheit nicht zum Tode. 1955.
Steig auf den Parnass, und schaue. 1960.
Im Sterben auferstehen. 1964.

Dramas

Der Auszug aus Ägypten / Die Manichäer. 1916.
Das Viergetier, 1920.
Hieram und Salomo, 1925.
Der Chef des Generalstabs. 1927.
Der Sturz des Antichrist. 1928.
Das Todeserlebnis des Manes. 1934.
Adonis-Spiel / Eine Herbstesfeier. 1935.
Friedenstragödie. 1936.
Fahrt ins andere Land. 1938.
Pestalozzi. 1939.
Märtyrer. 1942.
Ruf am Abgrund. 1943.
Karoline von Günderrode. 1946.
Barrabas. 1949.
Alexanders Wandlung. 1953.
Lin. 1957.

Essays

Begegnungen mit Rudolf Steiner, 1926/1955.
Mani / Sein Leben und seine Lehre. 1930.
Goethes Geistgestalt. 1932.
Conrad Ferdinand Meyers Lebendige Gestalt. 1937.
Lebensbildnis Pestalozzis. 1939.
Die Krisis im Leben des Künstlers. 1922.
Der Künstler zwischen Westen und Osten. 1925.
Der Künstler und die Erfüllung der Mysterien. 1928.
Dramaturgische Beiträge zu den Schönen Wissenschaften.
    1935.
Frührot der Mysteriendichtung. 1940.
Geistige Heimat. 1941.
Krisis, Katharsis, Therapie im Geistesleben der
    Gegenwart. 1944.
Vorhut des Geistes. 1945.
Wiedergeburt der Schönen Wissenschaften. 1946.
Mysterienflug. 1948.
Geist-Erkenntnis / Gottes-Liebe. 1949.
Dichtung als Weg zur Einweihung. 1960.
Brennende Probleme. 1956.

ALBERT STEFFEN

World literary judgment may well consider Albert Steffen,
distinguished Swiss poet, dramatist, novelist and essayist, as
one of the greatest literary figures of the twentieth century.

He was born in 1884 and died on July 15, 1963, the author of
over seventy volumes of published works.

"...There is no moral narrowness, no sitting in judgment, no
lack of understanding in the poet's view. Life is to him not a
mere spectacle of nature, but rather eternal doing, struggling
and suffering of that highest faculty of love in the conquest
and meaningfulness of which he believes."

Hermann Hesse

"After reading Albert Steffen's books, one feels cleaner and
better and this effect alone is so rare in the work of a writer
and poet, that it gives to it a special significance."

Dr. Robert Faesi — (Hon. Prof. — Univ. for
Modern German Lit., Zurich)

"...His words play in a convincing way between the spheres of
spirit and of the senses, so that we may experience this poet as
thoroughly modern, but in addition — and this distinguishes
him from many others — true and genuine in every fiber.

Dr. Walter Muschg
(author of "Von Trakl Zu Brecht")

ABOUT THE
TRANSLATOR

Daisy Aldan is a renowned poet, novelist and translator. Her awards include, among others, the Alta (American Literary Translators Award) from the University of Texas, the DeWitt American Lyric Poetry Award, the Rochester Festival of the Arts, First prize for poetry, and her work is being collected by the Beinecke Rare Book and Manuscript Library at Yale University. Her translations include works by Rudolf Steiner, and Herbert Witzenmann, *Selected Poems* of Albert Steffen (from German), *To Purify the Words of the Tribe: Complete Verse Poems* of Stéphane Mallarmé, (from French) and *Selected Poems* of Edith Södergran (from Swedish). Most recent books are *Day of the Wounded Eagle* (a Novella), and *In Passage*, (Poetry), both nominated for Pulitzer Prizes.

TRANSLATIONS INTO ENGLISH OF WORKS BY ALBERT STEFFEN BY DAISY ALDAN

BARRABAS, a verse play set in Jerusalem at the time of the Crucifixion.

CLIMB PARNASSUS, AND BEHOLD, one of the last volumes of poetry composed by Albert Steffen before his death in 1963.

ON THE MYSTERIES OF ELEUSIS, an essay describing the annual celebration at the Mystery Center of Eleusis in Ancient Greece.

SELECTED POEMS OF ALBERT STEFFEN, from various volumes of Steffen's poetry.

THE DEATH EXPERIENCE OF MANES, a verse play dealing with the Manichaeans.